MW00914193

PROJECTS for BABY

Made with the Knook™   { now you can **knit** with a **crochet hook**! }

From cute hats and a sweater to three cozy blankets, all these precious baby gifts can
be knitted with your choice of the Knook™ or traditional needles. Light weight yarns
make them ultra soft, and our online technique video support makes them extra easy.

2

9

12

15

18

22

LEISURE ARTS, INC. • Maumelle, Arkansas

Garter Sweater - Knook

 **EASY**

SHOPPING LIST

Yarn (Light Weight) 🌀 LIGHT 3

[5 ounces, 459 yards (141 grams, 420 meters) per skein]:

- ☐ Green - 1{1-2} skein(s)
- ☐ Yellow - 30 yards (27.5 meters)

Knook

- ☐ Size G (4 mm) **or** size needed for gauge

Additional Supplies

- ☐ Extra Knook cords - 2
- ☐ ⅝" (16 mm) Button
- ☐ Large snap
- ☐ Sewing needle and matching thread
- ☐ Tapestry needle

SIZE INFORMATION

Size: 3 to 6 Months

{12 to18 Months-24 Months}

Finished Chest Measurement:

17½{19½-21½}"/44.5{49.5-54.5} cm

Size Note: We have printed the instructions in different colors to make it easier for you to find:

- 3-6 Months in Blue
- 12-18 Months in Pink
- 24 Months in Green

Instructions in Black apply to all sizes.

GAUGE INFORMATION

In Garter Stitch (knit each row),

23 sts and 52 rows = 4" (10 cm)

The sweater is worked in one piece, beginning at the Back bottom edge, picking up stitches for the Sleeves, then working up and over the shoulders to end at the Fronts bottom edges. The Right Front & Sleeve will be left on an extra Knook cord while you work the Left Front & Sleeve *(see page 8 for schematic).*

BUTTONHOLE

Bring yarn to **front** *(pink yarn used for clarity)*, slip next st as if to **purl** *(Fig. 1a)*, bring yarn to **back**, slip next st as if to **purl** and pull through first st on Knook *(Fig. 1b)*, bring yarn to **front**, slip next st as if to **purl** and pull through first st on Knook, bring yarn to **back**, slip next st as if to **purl** and pull through first st on Knook; ch 5, pull loop on Knook through first st on Knook *(Fig. 1c)*, pick up 4 sts across ch *(Fig. 1d)*.

Fig. 1a

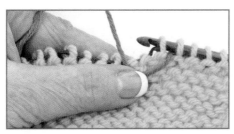

Fig. 1b

Fig. 1c

Fig. 1d

Before working a chain at the beginning of a row to add new stitches; turn, pull the cord out of the row below, then unthread the cord from the Knook, leaving the stitches on the cord. Thread the Knook with a second cord *(Fig. 2)* to use while picking up stitches across chain. Remove extra cord when no longer needed.

Fig. 2

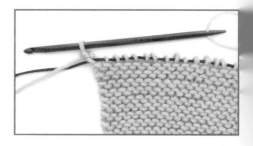

Sleeves & Neck

Rows 1 and 2: Ch 37{47-51}, pick up 36{46-50} sts across ch, knit across, pull extra cord out of row below: 124{150-164} sts.

One extra ch was made on each side to replace the edge sts on the Back used to begin each ch.

Knit each row until piece measures approximately 8⅞{9¾-10½}"/ 22.5{25-26.5} cm from foundation ch edge, ending by working a **wrong** side row.

INSTRUCTIONS
Back

With Green, ch 52{58-64}.

Foundation Row (Right side)**:** Pick up 51{57-63} sts on foundation ch: 52{58-64} sts.

Note: Loop a short piece of yarn around any stitch to mark Foundation Row as **right** side.

Row 1: Knit across.

Knit each row until piece measures approximately 5⅜{5¾-6¼}"/ 13.5{14.5-16} cm from foundation ch edge, ending by working a **wrong** side row.

At end of last row, turn; pull cord out of the row below, unthread Knook, leaving sts on cord. Thread Knook with extra cord to work Dividing Row.

Dividing Row: K 50{60-67}, pull Knook thru the sts, 📹 unthread the cord from Knook, pull first cord out of row below sts just worked and thread Knook with end of first cord, bind off next 24{30-30} sts (Back Neck), knit across: 50{60-67} sts on **each** cord.

Left Front & Sleeve

Rows 1-13: Knit across.

Row 14: Ch 18{23-23}, pick up 17{22-22} sts across ch (Left Front Neck), knit across: 67{82-89} sts.

One extra ch was made to replace Front st used to begin ch.

Knit each row until piece measures approximately 12³/₈{13¾-14¾}"/ 31{35-37.5} cm from foundation ch edge, ending by working a **right** side row.

Next Row: Bind off 36{46-50} sts (Left Sleeve finished), knit across: 31{36-39} sts.

Knit each row until piece measures approximately 17¾{19½-21}"/ 45{49.5-53.5} cm from foundation ch edge, ending by working a **right** side row.

Bind off all sts in **knit**.

Right Front & Sleeve

With **wrong** side facing, thread the Knook with the neck edge end of the remaining cord.

Rows 1-12: Knit across: 50{60-67} sts.

Row 13: Ch 18{23-23}, pick up 17{22-22} sts across ch (Right Front Neck), knit across: 67{82-89} sts.

One extra ch was made to replace Front st used to begin ch.

Knit each row until piece measures approximately 12³/₈{13¾-14¾}"/ 31{35-37.5} cm from foundation ch edge, ending by working a **wrong** side row.

Next Row: Bind off 36{46-50} sts (Right Sleeve finished), knit across: 31{36-39} sts.

Knit each row until piece measures approximately 17¾{19½-21}"/ 45{49.5-53.5} cm from foundation ch edge, ending by working a **right** side row.

Bind off all sts in **knit**.

Finishing

With **right** side facing and beginning at bottom edge, 📹 weave side and underarm in one continuous seam *(Fig. 17, page 31)*.

BUTTONHOLE BAND

Girl's: With **right** side of Right Front facing and Yellow, 📹 pick up 45{50-54} sts evenly spaced across *(Fig. 10, page 28)*.

Boy's: With **right** side of Left Front facing and Yellow, 📹 pick up 45{50-53} sts evenly spaced across *(Fig. 10, page 28)*.

Rows 1-4: Knit across.

Girl's Row 5: K2, work Buttonhole, knit across.

Boy's Row 5: Knit across to last 5 sts, work Buttonhole, K1.

Rows 6-8: Knit across.

Bind off all sts in **knit**.

Sew button to Front opposite Buttonhole.

Sew ball side of snap to corner of same Front as button and sew socket side of snap to opposite Front.

Garter Sweater - Knit

 **EASY**

SHOPPING LIST

Yarn (Light Weight) **LIGHT 3**

[5 ounces, 459 yards (141 grams, 420 meters) per skein]:

☐ Green - 1{1-2} skein(s)

☐ Yellow - 30 yards (27.5 meters)

Knitting Needles

Straight knitting needles,

☐ Size 6 (4 mm) **or** size needed for gauge

Additional Supplies

☐ ⁵/₈" (16 mm) Button

☐ Large snap

☐ Sewing needle and matching thread

☐ Tapestry needle

SIZE INFORMATION

Size: 3 to 6 Months

{12 to 18 Months-24 Months}

Finished Chest Measurement:

17½{19½-21½}"/44.5{49.5-54.5} cm

Size Note: We have printed the instructions in different colors to make it easier for you to find:

• 3 to 6 Months in Blue

• 12 to 18 Months in Pink

• 24 Months in Green

Instructions in Black apply to all sizes.

GAUGE INFORMATION

In Garter Stitch (knit each row),

23 sts and 52 rows = 4" (10 cm)

TECHNIQUE USED

Adding New Stitches

(Figs. 13a & b, page 30)

The sweater is worked in one piece, beginning at the Back bottom edge, adding on stitches for the Sleeves, then working up and over the shoulders to end at the Fronts bottom edges.

INSTRUCTIONS
Back

With Green, cast on 52{58-64} sts.

Row 1 (Right side): Knit across.

Note: Loop a short piece of yarn around any stitch to mark Row 1 as **right** side.

Knit each row until piece measures approximately $5^3/_8${5¾-6¼}"/ 13.5{14.5-16} cm from cast on edge, ending by working a **wrong** side row.

Sleeves & Neck

Rows 1 and 2: Add on 36{46-50} sts, knit across: 124{150-164} sts.

Knit each row until piece measures approximately $8^7/_8${9¾-10½}"/ 22.5{25-26.5} cm from cast on edge, ending by working a **wrong** side row.

Each side of Neck will be worked at the same time using separate yarn for **each** side.

Next Row (Dividing row): K 50{60-67}; with second yarn, bind off next 24{30-30} sts (Back Neck), knit across: 50{60-67} sts **each** side.

Fronts

Rows 1-13: Knit across; with second yarn, knit across.

Row 14: Knit across; with second yarn, add on 17{22-22} sts (Left Front Neck), knit across.

Row 15: Knit across; with second yarn, add on 17{22-22} sts (Right Front Neck), knit across: 67{82-89} sts **each** side.

Knit each row until piece measures approximately $12^3/_8${13¾-14¾}"/ 31{35-37.5} cm from cast on edge, ending by working a **right** side row.

Next 2 Rows: Bind off 36{46-50} sts (Sleeve finished), knit across; with second yarn, knit across: 31{36-39} sts **each** Front.

Knit each row until piece measures approximately 17¾{19½-21}"/ 45{49.5-53.5} cm from cast on edge, ending by working a **right** side row.

Bind off all sts in **knit**.

7

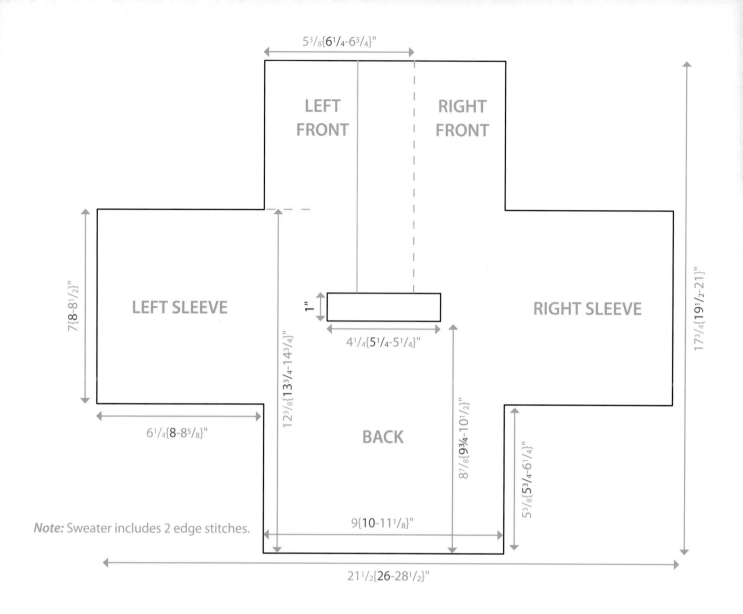

5³/₈{6¹/₄-6³/₄}"

LEFT FRONT

RIGHT FRONT

17³/₄{19¹/₂-21}"

LEFT SLEEVE

7{8-8¹/₂}"

1"

RIGHT SLEEVE

4¹/₄{5¹/₄-5¹/₄}"

12³/₈{13³/₄-14³/₄}"

6¹/₄{8-8⁵/₈}"

BACK

8⁷/₈{9³/₄-10¹/₂}"

5³/₈{5³/₄-6¹/₄}"

Note: Sweater includes 2 edge stitches.

9{10-11¹/₈}"

21¹/₂{26-28¹/₂}"

Finishing

📹 Weave side and underarm in one continuous seam *(Fig. 17, page 31)*.

BUTTONHOLE BAND

Girl's: With **right** side of Right Front facing and Yellow,
📹 pick up 45{50-54} sts evenly spaced across *(Fig. 16, page 31)*.

Boy's: With **right** side of Left Front facing and Yellow,
📹 pick up 45{50-54} sts evenly spaced across *(Fig. 16, page 31)*.

Rows 1-4: Knit across.

Girl's Row 5: K2, bind off next 3 sts, knit across.

Boy's Row 5: Knit across to last 5 sts, bind off next 3 sts, K1.

Row 6: Knit across to bound off sts, add on 3 sts, knit across.

Rows 7 and 8: Knit across.

Bind off all sts in **knit**.

Sew button to Front opposite Buttonhole. Sew ball side of snap to corner of same Front as button and sew socket side of snap to opposite Front.

Baby Beret

Shown on page 11.

 **EASY**

SHOPPING LIST

Yarn (Light Weight)

[4.25 ounces, 310 yards (120 grams, 283 meters) per skein]:

☐ 73{99} yards [67{90.5} meters]

Knook

☐ Size E (3.5 mm) **or** size needed for gauge

OR

Knitting Needles

Double pointed (set of 5),

☐ Size 4 (3.5 mm) **or** size needed for gauge

Additional Supplies

☐ Split-ring marker

☐ Tapestry needle

SIZE INFORMATION

Sizes: 0 to 3 Months {6 to 12 Months}

Finished Circumference:

13¼{14½}"/33.5{37} cm

Size Note: We have printed the instructions for the sizes in different colors to make it easier for you to find:

• Size 0 to 3 Months in Blue

• Size 6 to 12 Months in Pink

Instructions in Black apply to both sizes.

GAUGE INFORMATION

In K2, P2 ribbing,

24 sts and 30 rnds = 4" (10 cm)

In Stockinette Stitch (knit each round),

22 sts and 30 rnds = 4" (10 cm)

TECHNIQUES USED

Knook M1 *(Figs. 7a & b, page 27)*

Knook K2 tog *(Figs. 8a & b, page 28)*

Knit M1 *(Figs. 12a & b, page 30)*

Knit K2 tog *(Fig. 14, page 30)*

INSTRUCTIONS
Ribbing

Knook: Ch 79{87}; ▣ bring first ch around to meet last ch made and being careful **not** to twist ch, pick up a st in first ch and in each ch around *(see Circular Knitting, page 27)*. ▣ Place marker around first st to indicate beginning of rnd *(see Markers, page 26)*: 80{88} sts.

Knitting Needles: Cast on 80{88} sts; placing 20{22} sts onto each needle, ▣ place marker around first st to indicate beginning of rnd *(see Using Double Pointed Needles, page 29)*.

Rnds 1-11: (K2, P2) around:

Body

Rnd 1: (K2, M1) around: 120{132} sts.

Rnds 2 thru 14{20}: Knit around.

Top Shaping

Rnd 1: ★ K 18{20}, K2 tog; repeat from ★ around: 114{126} sts.

Rnd 2 AND ALL EVEN NUMBERED RNDS THROUGH RND 14: Knit around.

Rnd 3: ★ K 17{19}, K2 tog; repeat from ★ around: 108{120} sts.

Rnd 5: ★ K 16{18}, K2 tog; repeat from ★ around: 102{114} sts.

Rnd 7: ★ K 15{17}, K2 tog; repeat from ★ around: 96{108} sts.

Rnd 9: ★ K 14{16}, K2 tog; repeat from ★ around: 90{102} sts.

Rnd 11: ★ K 13{15}, K2 tog; repeat from ★ around: 84{96} sts.

Rnd 13: ★ K 12{14}, K2 tog; repeat from ★ around: 78{90} sts.

Rnd 15: ★ K 11{13}, K2 tog; repeat from ★ around: 72{84} sts.

Rnd 16: ★ K 10{12}, K2 tog; repeat from ★ around: 66{78} sts.

Rnd 17: ★ K9{11}, K2 tog; repeat from ★ around: 60{72} sts.

Rnd 18: ★ K8{10}, K2 tog; repeat from ★ around: 54{66} sts.

Rnd 19: ★ K7{9}, K2 tog; repeat from ★ around: 48{60} sts.

Rnd 20: ★ K6{8}, K2 tog; repeat from ★ around: 42{54} sts.

Rnd 21: ★ K5{7}, K2 tog; repeat from ★ around: 36{48} sts.

Rnd 22: ★ K4{6}, K2 tog; repeat from ★ around: 30{42} sts.

Rnd 23: ★ K3{5}, K2 tog; repeat from ★ around: 24{36} sts.

Rnd 24: ★ K2{4}, K2 tog; repeat from ★ around: 18{30} sts.

Rnd 25: ★ K1{3}, K2 tog; repeat from ★ around: 12{24} sts.

Size 6 to 12 Months ONLY

Rnd 26: (K2, K2 tog) around: 18 sts.

Rnd 27: (K1, K2 tog) around: 12 sts.

Both Sizes

Last Rnd: K2 tog around: 6 sts.

Cut yarn, leaving an 8" (20.5 cm) length for sewing.

▣ **Knook:** Thread tapestry needle with end and slip remaining stitches from cord onto needle; remove cord. Pull **tightly** to close and secure end.

▣ **Knitting Needles:** Thread tapestry needle with end and slip remaining stitches from knitting needles onto tapestry needle. Pull **tightly** to close and secure end.

Baby Hat

EASY

Finished Size:

Fits 12" (30.5 cm) head circumference

SHOPPING LIST

Yarn (Super Fine Weight) SUPER FINE **1**

[1.75 ounces, 239 yards (50 grams, 218 meters) per skein]:

☐ 1 skein

Knook

☐ Size E (3.5 mm) **or** size needed for gauge

OR

Knitting Needles

Double pointed (set of 5),

☐ Size 4 (3.5 mm) **or** size needed for gauge

Additional Supplies

☐ Split-ring marker

☐ Tapestry needle

GAUGE INFORMATION

In Stockinette Stitch (knit each round),

28 sts and 44 rnds = 4" (10 cm)

TECHNIQUE USED

 Knook K2 tog
(Figs. 8a & b, page 28)

 Knit K2 tog *(Fig. 14, page 30)*

INSTRUCTIONS
Body

Knook: Ch 79;  bring first ch around to meet last ch made and being careful **not** to twist ch, pick up a st in first ch and in each ch around *(see Circular Knitting, page 27)*.
 Place marker **around first st** to indicate beginning of rnd *(see Markers, page 26)*: 80 sts.

Knitting Needles: Cast on 80 sts; placing 20 sts onto each needle,  place marker **around first st to** indicate beginning of rnd *(see Using Double Pointed Needles, page 29)*.

Knit each rnd until Hat measures 4½" (11.5 cm) from foundation ch/cast on edge.

Top Shaping

Rnd 1: (K8, K2 tog) around: 72 sts.

Rnd 2 AND ALL EVEN NUMBERED RNDS: Knit around.

Rnd 3: (K7, K2 tog) around: 64 sts.

Rnd 5: (K6, K2 tog) around: 56 sts.

Rnd 7: (K5, K2 tog) around: 48 sts.

Rnd 9: (K4, K2 tog) around: 40 sts.

Rnd 11: (K3, K2 tog) around: 32 sts.

Rnd 13: (K2, K2 tog) around: 24 sts.

Rnd 15: (K1, K2 tog) around: 16 sts.

Rnd 16: K2 tog around: 8 sts.

Cut yarn, leaving an 8" (20.5 cm) length for sewing.

 **Knook:** Thread tapestry needle with end and slip remaining stitches from cord onto tapestry needle; remove cord. Pull **tightly** to close and secure end.

 **Knitting Needles:** Thread tapestry needle with end and slip remaining stitches from knitting needles onto tapestry needle. Pull **tightly** to close and secure end.

Tracks & Trails Afghan

Shown on page 17.

 **EASY**

Finished Size:

36" x 41¾" (91.5 cm x 106 cm)

SHOPPING LIST

Yarn (Light Weight) **[LIGHT 3]**

[4 ounces, 242 yards

(113 grams, 222 meters) per skein]:

☐ 6 skeins

Knook

☐ Size G (4 mm) **or** size needed for gauge

OR

Knitting Needle

36" (91.5 cm) Circular,

☐ Size 6 (4 mm) **or** size needed for gauge

GAUGE INFORMATION

In pattern, 21 sts and 24 rows = 4" (10 cm)

INSTRUCTIONS

Knook: Ch 188; pick up 187 sts across foundation ch: 188 sts.

Knitting Needle: Cast on 188 sts.

Rows 1-6: Knit across.

Row 7: K4, purl across to last 4 sts, K4.

Row 8 (Right side)**:** K7, P3, (K 15, P3) across to last 16 sts, K 16.

Row 9: K4, P 12, K3, (P 15, K3) across to last 7 sts, P3, K4.

Rows 10 and 11: Repeat Rows 8 and 9.

Row 12: K7, P 15, (K3, P 15) across to last 4 sts, K4.

Row 13: K 19, P3, (K 15, P3) across to last 4 sts, K4.

Rows 14 and 15: K7, P 15, (K3, P 15) across to last 4 sts, K4.

Row 16: K 19, P3, (K 15, P3) across to last 4 sts, K4.

Row 17: K7, P 15, (K3, P 15) across to last 4 sts, K4.

Row 18: K4, P 12, K3, (P 15, K3) across to last 7 sts, P3, K4.

Row 19: K7, P3, (K 15, P3) across to last 16 sts, K 16.

Row 20: K4, P 12, K3, (P 15, K3) across to last 7 sts, P3, K4.

Row 21: K4, P6, K3, (P 15, K3) across to last 13 sts, P9, K4.

Row 22: K 13, P3, (K 15, P3) across to last 10 sts, K 10.

Rows 23 and 24: K4, P6, K3, (P 15, K3) across to last 13 sts, P9, K4.

Rows 25 and 26: Repeat Rows 22 and 23.

Row 27: K4, P 12, K3, (P 15, K3) across to last 7 sts, P3, K4.

Row 28: K7, P3, (K 15, P3) across to last 16 sts, K 16.

Row 29: K4, P 12, K3, (P 15, K3) across to last 7 sts, P3, K4.

Rows 30-245: Repeat Rows 12-29, 12 times.

Rows 246-250: Knit across.

Bind off all sts in **knit**.

Cable Baby Blanket

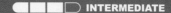 **INTERMEDIATE**

Finished Size:

32¾" wide x 37" long (83 cm x 94 cm)

SHOPPING LIST

Yarn (Light Weight) [LIGHT 3]

[5 ounces, 362 yards (140 grams, 331 meters) per skein]:

- ☐ Pale Pink - 3 skeins
- ☐ Pink - 2 skeins

Knook

- ☐ Size E (3.5 mm) **or** size needed for gauge

OR

Knitting Needles

Straight knitting needles,

- ☐ Size 4 (3.5 mm) **or** size needed for gauge

Additional Supplies

- ☐ Tapestry needle
- ☐ Cable needle (Knitting needles version only)

GAUGE INFORMATION

In Basketweave pattern,

> 24 sts and 28 rows = 4" (10 cm)

In Cable pattern,

> Each Panel = 2¾" (7 cm) wide
>
> One repeat (24 rows) = 3" (7.5 cm)

KNOOK STITCH GUIDE

CABLE 6 BACK *(abbreviated C6B)* (uses next 6 sts)

Skip next 3 sts, pull skipped sts to **back** of work on cord *(skipped sts shown in yellow for clarity, Fig. 3a)*, knit next 3 sts *(Fig. 3b)*, then knit 3 skipped sts.

Fig. 3a

Fig. 3b

RIGHT TWIST (uses next 4 sts)

Skip next 3 sts, pull skipped sts to **front** of work on cord *(skipped sts shown in yellow for clarity)*, purl next st *(Fig. 4a)*, then knit 3 skipped sts *(Fig. 4b)*.

Fig. 4a

Fig. 4b

LEFT TWIST (uses next 4 sts)

Skip next st, pull skipped st to **back** of work on cord *(skipped st shown in yellow for clarity)*, knit next 3 sts *(Fig. 5a)*, then purl skipped st *(Fig. 5b)*.

Fig. 5a

Fig. 5b

KNIT STITCH GUIDE

CABLE 6 BACK

(abbreviated C6B)

(uses next 6 sts)

Slip next 3 sts onto cable needle and hold in **back** of work, K3 sts from left needle, K3 from cable needle.

RIGHT TWIST (uses next 4 sts)

Slip next 3 sts onto cable needle and hold in **front** of work, P1 from left needle, K3 from cable needle.

LEFT TWIST (uses next 4 sts)

Slip next st onto cable needle and hold in **back** of work, K3 from left needle, P1 from cable needle.

INSTRUCTIONS
Basketweave Panel
(Make 4)

Knook: With Pale Pink, ch 40; pick up 39 sts on foundation ch: 40 sts.

Knitting Needles: Cast on 40 sts.

Rows 1-5: (K4, P4) across.

Rows 6-10: (P4, K4) across.

Rows 11-260: Repeat Rows 1-10, 25 times.

Bind off all sts in **knit**.

Cable Panel (Make 3)

Knook: With Pink, ch 22; pick up 21 sts on foundation ch: 22 sts.

Knitting Needles: Cast on 22 sts.

Row 1 (Right side)**:** K4, P4, K6, P4, K4.

Row 2: P4, K4, P6, K4, P4.

Row 3: K4, P4, C6B, P4, K4.

Row 4: P4, K4, P6, K4, P4.

Rows 5-8: Repeat Rows 1 and 2 twice.

Row 9: K4, P4, C6B, P4, K4.

Row 10: P4, K4, P6, K4, P4.

Row 11: K4, P3, Left Twist, Right Twist, P3, K4.

Row 12: P4, K3, P3, K2, P3, K3, P4.

Row 13: K4, P3, K3, P2, K3, P3, K4.

Rows 14-24: Repeat Rows 12 and 13, 5 times; then repeat Row 12 once **more**.

Row 25: K4, P3, Right Twist, Left Twist, P3, K4.

Row 26: P4, K4, P6, K4, P4.

Rows 27-298: Repeat Rows 3-26, 11 times; then repeat Rows 3-10 once **more**.

Bind off all sts in **knit**.

Assembly

Using photo as guide for placement, with **right** sides of Cable Panels facing, and bottom edges at same end, ▓ weave Panels together *(Fig. 17, page 31)*.

Mitered Squares Afghan

 **INTERMEDIATE**

Finished Size:

36" x 48" (91.5 cm x 122 cm)

SHOPPING LIST

Yarn (Light Weight) 🧶 3

[1.75 ounces, 161 yards (50 grams, 147 meters) per skein]:

☐ Red - 2 skeins

☐ Navy - 2 skeins

☐ Yellow - 2 skeins

☐ Green - 2 skeins

☐ Orange - 2 skeins

☐ Purple - 2 skeins

Knook

☐ Size H (5 mm) **or** size needed for gauge

OR

Knitting Needles

Straight knitting needles,

☐ Size 7 (4.5 mm) **or** size needed for gauge

Additional Supplies

☐ Split-ring marker

☐ Tapestry needle

GAUGE INFORMATION

In Garter Stitch, 20 sts = 4" (10 cm)

Small Square = 6" (15.25 cm) square

Large Square = 12" (30.5 cm) square

TECHNIQUE USED

📹 Knook Slip 1 as if to **knit**, K2 tog, PSSO *(Figs. 9a & b, page 28)*

📹 Knit Slip 1 as if to **knit**, K2 tog, PSSO *(Figs. 15a & b, page 31)*

INSTRUCTIONS
Small Square
(Make 24 - 4 each color)

Knook: Ch 61, pick up 60 sts on foundation ch: 61 sts.

Knitting Needles: Cast on 61 sts.

Row 1 (Right side): K 29, slip 1 as if to **knit**, K2 tog, PSSO, 📹 place split-ring marker around st just made *(see Markers, page 26)*, K 29: 59 sts.

Row 2: Knit across.

Row 3: Knit across to within one st of marker, slip 1 as if to **knit**, K2 tog, PSSO, move marker to st just made, knit across: 57 sts.

Rows 4-57: Repeat Rows 2 and 3, 27 times: 3 sts.

Row 58: Slip 1 as if to **knit**, K2 tog, PSSO; cut yarn and pull through last st.

Large Square
(Make 6 - 1 each color)

Knook: Ch 121, pick up 120 sts on foundation ch: 121 sts.

Knitting Needles: Cast on 121 sts.

Row 1 (Right side): K 59, slip 1 as if to **knit**, K2 tog, PSSO, place split-ring marker around st just made, knit across: 119 sts.

Row 2: Knit across.

Row 3: Knit across to within one st of marker, slip 1 as if to **knit**, K2 tog, PSSO, move marker to st just made, knit across: 117 sts.

Rows 4-117: Repeat Rows 2 and 3, 57 times: 3 sts.

Row 118: Slip 1 as if to **knit**, K2 tog, PSSO; cut yarn and pull through last st.

Assembly

Using Placement Diagram as a guide, place all Squares with foundation ch or cast on edge in the same direction. With **right** sides together, and using corresponding color yarn, sew Squares together.

General Instructions

ABBREVIATIONS

C6B	Cable 6 Back
ch(s)	chain(s)
cm	centimeters
K	knit
mm	millimeters
M1	Make one
P	purl
PSSO	pass slipped stitch over
Rnd(s)	round(s)
st(s)	stitch(es)
tog	together

SYMBOLS & TERMS

★ — work instructions following ★ as many **more** times as indicated in addition to the first time.

( ) or [ ] — work enclosed instructions as many times as specified by the number immediately following **or** contains explanatory remarks.

colon (:) — the number(s) given after a colon at the end of a row or round denote(s) the number of stitches you should have on that row or round.

GAUGE

Exact gauge is **essential** for proper size or fit. Before beginning your project, make a sample swatch using the yarn and Knook/needles specified. After completing the swatch, measure it, counting your stitches and rows carefully. If your swatch is larger or smaller, **make another, changing the Knook/needle size to get the correct gauge.** Keep trying until you find the size Knook/needles that will give you the specified gauge.

MARKERS

As a convenience to you, we have used markers to indicate the beginning of a round or to mark the placement of decreases. Place markers as indicated. When using a split-ring marker, move it up at the end of each round. Remove it when no longer needed.

KNIT / KNOOK TERMINOLOGY	
UNITED STATES	**INTERNATIONAL**
gauge =	tension
bind off =	cast off
yarn over (YO) =	yarn forward (yfwd) **or** yarn around needle (yrn)

■□□□ **BEGINNER**	Projects for first-time knitters using basic knit and purl stitches. Minimal shaping.
■■□□ **EASY**	Projects using basic stitches, repetitive stitch patterns, simple color changes, and simple shaping and finishing.
■■■□ **INTERMEDIATE**	Projects with a variety of stitches, such as basic cables and lace, simple intarsia, double-pointed needles and knitting in the round needle techniques, mid-level shaping and finishing.
■■■■ **EXPERIENCED**	Projects using advanced techniques and stitches, such as short rows, fair isle, more intricate intarsia, cables, lace patterns, and numerous color changes.

KNOOK TECHNIQUES
Circular Knitting

Chain the required number of stitches. Bring the first chain around to meet the last chain made, making sure that the chain isn't twisted *(Fig. 6a)*.

Fig. 6a

Begin by picking up a stitch in the first chain *(Fig. 6b)* and in each chain around. Remember the loop on the Knook counts as your first stitch.

Fig. 6b

KNOOK INCREASES
Make One *(abbreviated M1)*

With yarn in **back**, insert the Knook under the horizontal strand between the stitches from the **back** to the **front** *(Fig. 7a)*, then knit into that strand *(Fig. 7b)*.

Fig. 7a

Fig. 7b

Yarn Weight Symbol & Names	LACE 0	SUPER FINE 1	FINE 2	LIGHT 3	MEDIUM 4	BULKY 5	SUPER BULKY 6
Type of Yarns in Category	Fingering, size 10 crochet thread	Sock, Fingering, Baby	Sport, Baby	DK, Light Worsted	Worsted, Afghan, Aran	Chunky, Craft, Rug	Bulky, Roving
Knit Gauge Range* in Stockinette St to 4" (10 cm)	33-40** sts	27-32 sts	23-26 sts	21-24 sts	16-20 sts	12-15 sts	6-11 sts
Advised Needle Size Range	000-1	1 to 3	3 to 5	5 to 7	7 to 9	9 to 11	11 and larger
Knook Gauge Ranges in Stockinette St to 4" (10 cm)		27-32 sts	23-26 sts	21-24 sts	16-20 sts	12-15 sts	6-11 sts
Advised Knook Size Range		B-1 to D-3	D-3 to F-5	F-5 to G-6	G-6 to I-9	I-9 to K-10½	M-13 and larger

*GUIDELINES ONLY: The chart above reflects the most commonly used gauges and needle sizes for specific yarn categories.

** Lace weight yarns are usually knitted on larger needles to create lacy openwork patterns. Accordingly, a gauge range is difficult to determine. Always follow the gauge stated in your pattern.

KNOOK DECREASES
Knit 2 Together

(abbreviated K2 tog)

Insert the Knook into the **front** of the second and then the first stitch on the cord as if to **knit** *(Fig. 8a)*, then knit them together as if they were one stitch *(Fig. 8b)*.

Fig. 8a

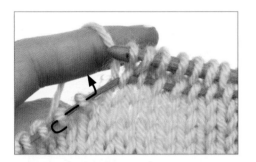

Fig. 8b

Slip 1, Knit 2 Together, Pass Slipped Stitch Over

(abbreviated slip 1, K2 tog, PSSO)

Slip one stitch as if to **knit** *(Fig. 9a)*, then knit the next two stitches together *(Figs. 8a & b)*. Pull the stitch just made through the slipped stitch *(Fig. 9b)*.

Fig. 9a

Fig. 9b

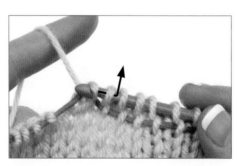

PICKING UP STITCHES

When instructed to pick up stitches on a knitted piece, insert the Knook from the **front** to the **back** at the edge *(Fig. 10)*. Catch the yarn as if picking up stitches on the foundation chain and draw the loop through, resulting in a stitch on the Knook. Repeat this along the edge, picking up the required number of stitches.

Fig. 10

KNITTING NEEDLES		
UNITED STATES	ENGLISH U.K.	METRIC (mm)
0	13	2
1	12	2.25
2	11	2.75
3	10	3.25
4	9	3.5
5	8	3.75
6	7	4
7	6	4.5
8	5	5
9	4	5.5
10	3	6
10½	2	6.5
11	1	8
13	00	9
15	000	10
17	---	12.75
19	---	15
35	---	19
50	---	25

KNIT TECHNIQUES
Using Double Pointed Needles

Divide the cast on stitches into fourths and place them onto each of 4 double pointed needles to form a square *(Fig. 11a)*.

Fig. 11a

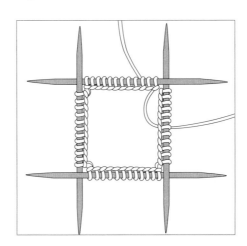

Place a marker around first st and with the fifth needle, work across the stitches on the first needle *(Fig. 11b)*. You will now have an empty needle with which to work the stitches from the next needle. Work the first stitch of each needle firmly to prevent gaps. Continue working around without turning the work.

Fig. 11b

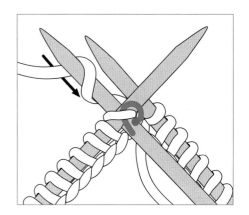

KNIT INCREASES
Make One *(abbreviated M1)*

Insert the left needle under the horizontal strand between the stitches from the **front** *(Fig. 12a)*. Then, knit into the **back** of the strand *(Fig. 12b)*.

Fig. 12a

Fig. 12b

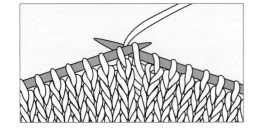

Adding New Stitches

Insert the right needle into the stitch as if to **knit**, yarn over and pull loop through *(Fig. 13a)*, insert the left needle into the loop just made from **front** to **back** and slip the loop onto the left needle *(Fig. 13b)*. Repeat for the required number of stitches.

Fig. 13a

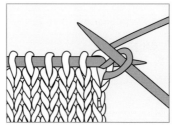

Fig. 13b

KNIT DECREASES
Knit 2 Together
(abbreviated K2 tog)

Insert the right needle into the **front** of the first two stitches as if to **knit** *(Fig. 14)*, then knit them together as if they were one stitch.

Fig. 14

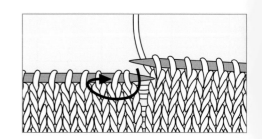

Slip 1, Knit 2 Together, Pass Slipped Stitch Over

(abbreviated slip 1, K2 tog, PSSO)

Slip one stitch as if to **knit** *(Fig. 15a)*, then knit the next two stitches together *(Fig. 14)*. With the left needle, bring the slipped stitch over the knit stitch *(Fig. 15b)* and off the needle.

Fig. 15a

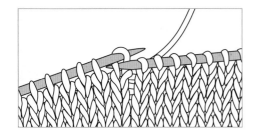

Fig. 15b

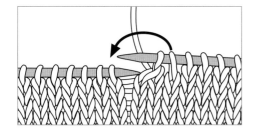

PICKING UP STITCHES

When instructed to pick up stitches, insert the needle from the **front** to the **back** under two strands at the edge of the piece *(Fig. 16)*. Put the yarn around the needle as if to **knit**, then bring the needle with the yarn through the stitch to the right side, resulting in a stitch on the needle. Repeat this along the edge, picking up the required number of stitches. A crochet hook may be helpful to pull the yarn through.

Fig. 16

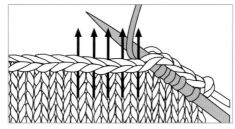

WEAVING SEAMS

With **right** side facing and edges even, sew through both pieces once to secure the beginning of the seam, leaving an ample yarn end to weave in later. Insert the needle under the bar **between** the first and second stitches on the row and pull the yarn through *(Fig. 17)*. Insert the needle under the next bar on the second side. Repeat from side to side, being careful to match the rows. If the edges are different lengths, it may be necessary to insert the needle under two bars at one edge.

Fig. 17

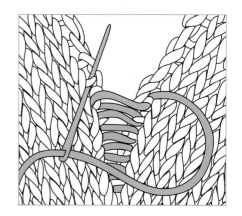

Yarn Information

Projects in this book were made with a variety of yarns. Any brand of the specified weight of yarn may be used. It is best to refer to the yardage/meters when determining how many balls or skeins of yarn to purchase. Remember, to arrive at the finished size, it is the GAUGE/TENSION that is important, not the brand of yarn. For your convenience, listed below are the specific yarns used to create our photography models.

GARTER SWEATER

Lion Brand® Babysoft® Yarn

Green - #170 Pistachio

Yellow - #160 Lemonade

BABY BERET

Bernat® Softee® Baby™

#31313 Pyjama Party

BABY HAT

Patons® Stretch Socks

#31222 Spearmint

TRACKS & TRAILS BLANKET

Red Heart® Baby TLC

#5046 Bunny

CABLE BABY BLANKET

Bernat® Softee® Baby ™

Pale Pink - #02001 Pink

Pink - #30205 Prettiest Pink

MITERED SQUARES AFGHAN

Patons® Astra™

Red - #02762 Cardinal

Navy - #02849 Navy

Yellow - #02941 School Bus Yellow

Green - #02708 Emerald

Orange - #08628 Hot Orange

Purple - #08317 Hot Lilac

Production Team: Writer/Technical Editor - Sarah J. Green; Editorial Writer - Susan Frantz Wiles; Senior Graphic Artist - Lora Puls; Graphic Artist - Becca Snider Tally; Photo Stylist - Lori Wenger; and Photographers - Jason Masters and Mark Mathews.

Instructions tested by Marianna Crowder, photo models made by Melanie Clark, Kelly Laux, Edith Smith, and Jennifer Snedecker.